Anne Bancroft has been a [...] religion and is the author o[...] including *Religions of the East, The Budd...* *The Spiritual Journey.*

'Classics of World Spirituality' series

The writings and teachings of the great spiritual masters are brought together in the *Vega Classics of World Spirituality* series. These volumes focus on the philosophical and religious meaning of the texts and their abiding relevance. They are introduced by internationally recognised scholars and spiritual leaders, who highlight and enhance the richness and depth of the writings.

Books in the series:

The Cloud of Unknowing
The Pilgrim's Progress
The Dhammapada
Rumi's Divan of Shems of Tabriz

Classics of World Spirituality

The
DHAMMAPADA

Introduced by
ANNE BANCROFT

First published by Element Books Ltd 1997
© Vega 2002
Introduction © Anne Bancroft

ISBN 1-84333-590-5

A catalogue record for this book is available
from the British Library

Published in 2002 by
Vega
64 Brewery Road
London, N7 9NT

A member of **Chrysalis** Books plc

Visit our website at www.chrysalisbooks.co.uk

Printed in Great Britain
by CPD, Wales
Cover design by Andrew Sutterby

Contents

Introduction

Introduction

The Dhammapada contains the most essential teachings of the Buddha. 'Dhamma' means teaching and 'pada' means path, so it is the path or way of the teaching. It is not all one lengthy discourse, but a compilation of what are said to be the Buddha's utterances over many years, brought together by his disciples to give the true nature of his unique understanding. The word 'Dhammapada' also means 'the Verses of the Law'. The Law is the Law of the universe. If we follow the Law we are in accord with the universe and happiness is the result. If we do not follow the Law, we feel at odds with ourselves and the world, and we suffer. These are simple truths, but very profound in their application. *The Dhammapada* is the way to understand them. For those who would like to investigate its source, it is a first century BC anthology which can be found in the Khuddaka-Nikaya (Shorter Discourses) section of the *Sutta Pitaka* (Basket of Discourses).

The sayings of the Buddha were recited orally for many years after his death in the fifth century BC. Although writing was practised during the Buddha's lifetime, the materials with which to write were precious, and using them for lengthy discourses was impractical. But the main reason for not writing them down was that Buddha's disciples were expected to remember his sayings; it is because they had to be learnt by rote that the teachings sometimes seem repetitive – they had to be held in the memory. Often they were chanted and the rhythm of the chant would fix the words in the mind. Chanting is a universal way of memorizing, and is still used in some branches of Buddhism today.

The Dhammapada came to be written down in the first century BC. It is one of the fifteen books of the Khuddaka-Nikaya and it is made up of 423 verses arranged by topic into 26 chapters. These verses are descriptions of the way to live, the life of meditation and the practice of reason and intelligence. There are many exhortations to cast off craving and orient yourself towards enlightenment, so it is not just a book of morality; it seeks to go further than that. Luckily the verses are easy to read and to memorize, and the many translations have given *The Dhammapada* worldwide popularity, representing for Buddhism what the *Bhagavad Gita* is for Hinduism and the *Tao Te Ching* is for Taoism.

During the 19th century the Buddhist teachings began to be translated into English by the Pali Text Society. The version of *The Dhammapada* that is presented here is based on that translation and also on other more modern versions; there are probably as many versions of *The Dhammapada* as of the *Tao Te Ching*. A list of the publications I consulted can be found in the Bibliography.

Because this book was first transcribed by monks from within a society in which women were not regarded as worthy of education, the language is sexually exclusive, referring only to men. This has been the style of even the modern versions, for inclusive language is a very recent development. Since I wanted to remain true to the text of *The Dhammapada* I have retained the pronoun 'he' where it is unavoidable, rather than replacing it with 'she' or 's/he'. Likewise, where a 'man' is referred to I have kept it, albeit reluctantly.

Turning to the background from which *The Dhammapada* arose, we can now ask: Who was the Buddha? He was an Indian prince of the Sakya clan who was born about 560 BC. His family ruled both a part of India that is now in Nepal and also part of North India itself. His family name was Gotama and his given name Siddhartha, but few people remember those. Just as Jesus of Nazareth became the Christ, the Anointed One of God, so Siddhartha became known throughout India – and, in time, the world – as the Buddha, the Awakened One. When people looked at him and saw his unusual quality, they would ask him: 'Are you a god?' 'No,' he would answer. 'Are you a magician?' 'No.' 'Are you a saint?' 'No.' 'Then, what are you?' 'I am awake.' Two other names have accompanied his popularity: Sakyamuni, the prophetic sage of the Sakyas; and a hauntingly mysterious title – Tathagata – the one who has finally come through. Or, more simply, the Enlightened One.

Growing up in the India of his day, the young Siddhartha would have been taught prayers from the *Vedas* and *Upanishads* and would have been affected by the yearning which pervades those prayers to transcend the realm of unstable and illusory life and become identified with the ultimate and timeless ground of all that is. One of the most popular prayers from the *Upanishads* reads:

> From the unreal lead me to the real;
> From darkness lead me to light;
> From death lead me to deathlessness.

It expresses the longing of the contemplative to throw off the confining limitations of the finite world and to find union with the infinite.

But against such a strong spiritual feeling, Siddhartha had to encounter his father's determination that his son should be a ruler, as he himself was; indeed, a far greater ruler, for he had plans that Siddhartha should become the emperor of all India. At that time wars were common between kingdoms and rival clans, and when Siddhartha was born a prophecy had been made that he would either become the great ruler, ending all strife, or that he would become a recluse, a wandering hermit.

The king naturally wanted his son to take his place in the world and, alarmed by the prophecy, he tried to see to it that Siddhartha was surrounded by every luxury and worldly pleasure. As soon as he was of the right age, he was married to his cousin and in due course a son was born. But Siddhartha grew more and more ill at ease amidst all the splendour of the court. Something essential was missing from his life, and undoubtedly the Upanishadic teaching helped him to see what it was.

In a famous sequence of events, the story relates that on successive journeys out of the palace Siddhartha saw four sights: a person bent double with age; a person lying down ill; a dead body being carried to the burning grounds, and a holy beggar, homeless and with nothing other than the robe he stood up in. He was ripe for the explosion which now took place within him. While such suffering existed in the world he could no longer insulate himself in the life of the court. Urgent questions formed in his mind. What was the true meaning of existence? What did death mean? What was the holy beggar hoping to find out? Why should suffering exist, and could there ever be a cure?

He was unable to remain in the palace, where so many false values were worshipped, and one night he secretly left for ever, donning the robe of a wandering beggar and setting forth into the forests to find the teachers he had heard of, sages who could perhaps show him the truths he sought.

But they could not. For six years he studied, and wandered from one sage to another, but no one could give him an answer to the real and ultimate question of what is the meaning of birth and death. At last he realized that the true answer lay within himself and was not to be found in any outside source. One night he decided to sit in contemplation beneath a forest tree, and to stay there until he knew the truth.

It is said that when the morning star appeared in the sky he experienced a great insight, and suddenly realized what those six years had failed to show him. He saw the origins of birth and death, he saw the infinity of the transcendent and its relationship to all existence, and he saw why mental suffering arises and how it can be cured. Awakened from his long

sleep, the sleep we all share, he was now the Buddha,
the fully enlightened one. It is said he spoke these
words on his enlightenment:

> Through countless weary lives I have sought the
> builder of this house and could not find him.
>   Now I have found you, O Builder, and never
> again shall you build this house. The rafters are
> snapped, the ridgepole is shattered. My mind has
> reached the end of craving and is free.

The Dhammapada: Old Age, verses 153, 154

For the rest of his life (he lived until the age of 80)
he walked the paths of India, teaching to whoever
would listen to him. He soon attracted followers who
wanted to share his understanding and in due course
a community of monks, the Sangha, was formed.
They were homeless and without possessions and
spent their days in teaching and meditation. An
order of nuns was established as well.

What was the core of the Buddha's teaching?
Certain basic principles were established from the
beginning. First there is the Void, or Emptiness –
not mere emptiness, but an absolute clarity and
transparency of consciousness. He believed that our
own consciousness, which is the necessary ground
of our experience, is a particular mode of the
ultimate Reality or Supreme Consciousness and is,
in essence, identical with it. That which is the basis
of the universe will be immeasurably more than
that which underlies human experience, and it is
the human destiny to move towards that greater
consciousness, which is also supreme happiness.
Such a spiritual quest, he believed, is always there

for each person to experience and he taught that
the true goal was to enter into that new state of
consciousness – Nirvana.

He believed that to understand that this *is*
the goal is essential for us at every level of life, for
otherwise life has no real meaning and we are filled
with vacancy and despair. 'There is,' he declared,
'an unborn, uncreated, unmade and unformed.
Were there not there would be no release from the
world of the born, created, made and formed.'

It was that release that the Buddha wanted to
make as plain as he could. He saw nothing mystical
or other-worldly in it; to him it was the natural and
totally desirable destination of all that lives, and his
outline of the path that could be taken towards it
was entirely practical.

As a background to that path, his followers
needed to understand that not only does 'the
unmade and the uncreated' (the Emptiness) pervade
and sustain every atom of the universe – so that, in
effect, we all live and move and have our being in it
– but that, in contrast, each material expression of
life, such as a human being, is conditioned and
'made'. Everybody has the basis of Emptiness, but
the particular self changes and is transformed every
day. We, in our 'thingness', are altogether relative
and not absolute. Each one of us is born, we live and
then we die, and although we think of the self as an
entity, in the Buddha's eyes it was not. Entities, as
such, do not exist, he said, and in that conclusion he
was uniquely modern, for it is the great discovery of
quantum physics in this century that nothing is
fixed; everything, including our bodies and minds,

is conditioned by, interacting with and co-dependent on everything else in the universe, including the stars.

> Everything is changing. It arises and passes away. The one who realizes this is freed from sorrow. This is the shining path.
>
> To exist is to know suffering. Realize this and be freed from suffering. This is the radiant path.
>
> There is no separate self to suffer. The one who understands this is free. This is the path of clarity.
>
> *The Dhammapada*: The Path, verses 277, 278, 279

All that is, said the Buddha, including ourselves, our thoughts and our feelings, is subject to change. Birth is change and death is change. There is nothing wrong with such a state, only with our attitudes towards it. We cling to life and try to possess it and make it our own. We crave for sensations such as happiness and hold on to them. Most of all, we attach to the feeling of 'I', the feeling of being a separate person. But it is this feeling more than any other which leads to trouble and suffering.

When a child is growing up it needs the perception of a self in order to recognize its world and experience relationships. A strong young ego is natural to the human animal. But when maturity is reached, the ego should give way to a deeper understanding of the nature of existence. When this does *not* happen the ego seems, in cancerous fashion, to grow large, no longer a natural by-product but a monstrous growth in its own right, feeding on its desire for separate existence.

Reality is distorted when the ego is not outgrown because then everything comes to be valued in accordance with the overwhelming need to keep the feeling of 'I' fed. The objects which feed it are clung to, and those which hurt it are avoided or fought. These two forces, clinging and avoidance, are the ones which bind man to suffering, said the Buddha. For karma, the law of cause and effect, ensures that every action has its result.

The way out of this dilemma is to cease to identify with the impermanent things of the world, and to identify instead with the changeless and formless unity which underlies every seemingly separate thing. Then we may realize that one's own self is not permanent or even central, and we can let go of it and accept the changeless within ourselves. The Buddha called this teaching *Anatta*, meaning to be empty of self. Many Hindus at the time were afraid of *Anatta*, believing it to mean annihilation, the end of consciousness, the losing of the known; and they did not have sufficient faith to believe that Emptiness would sustain them. Many people have the same fear today.

But the Buddha urged people to avoid the two extremes of either believing in a permanent self or believing that there is no self at all. What he taught was a middle way. Everything, he said, is in a state of becoming and there never exists one static moment when this becoming attains to something fixed. No sooner do we think we know ourselves by name and form than we have subtly changed. Life is a continuous stream of becoming, from before conception to after death.

Carl Jung once said that almost all the psychological problems brought to him were basically religious ones. People believe that the 'world of the born, created, made and formed' is all there is, and their ignorance of the 'unborn and uncreated' causes them to cling to all that is material, and to drown the hopelessness of this attitude in all sorts of addictions.

In response to this existential dilemma, the Buddha carefully laid out a path of growing awareness which would take the follower as gradually as he or she wished to a deeper understanding of existence. Nothing in this path depends on belief; all can be discovered by the senses, and thus there is no moment at which reassurance is not present.

First he gave four statements about human existence, which are known in Buddhism as the Four Noble Truths. In a similar way to a doctor, he stated first the presence of an illness in humanity; second the nature of that illness; third that it can be cured, and fourth the way to cure it.

These are the Four Noble Truths:

1   Life as we ordinarily live it is often full of unhappiness. As well as the pain of birth, old age, sickness and death, there is separation, grief and despair. At a less intense level there is anger, resentment and frustration, which often fill our minds to the exclusion of anything else.

2   The main cause of such unhappiness is craving – craving for pleasure, craving for individual existence and craving for release from our present situation.

3   Such craving can be transcended. We can liber-
ate ourselves from the demands of the insatiable
ego and find a way of life which leads to a supreme
happiness, Nirvana.

4   That way of life consists in eight steps, known in
Buddhism as the Eightfold Path.

> He who takes refuge in the Way and journeys with
> those who follow it, clearly sees the four great
> truths.
>   Suffering, the cause of suffering, the ceasing of
> suffering and the eightfold path that leads to the
> end of suffering.
>   Then at last he finds safety. He is delivered from
> suffering and is free.
>
> *The Dhammapada*: The Awakened One, verses
> 190, 191, 192

Here is the Eightfold Path:

1   Correct understanding. Without a proper
understanding of the nature of our problems we are
lost. It is essential that we look deeply into our
motives and needs.

2   Correct thinking. Much of what passes for
thought is in fact preconception and misunder-
standing based on prejudice. To think properly
demands objectivity and a settled purpose to
achieve a solution.

3   Correct speech. It is essential to refrain from
unkind gossip and lying and to cultivate ways
of communication which are constructive and
creative.

4   Correct conduct. To avoid being destructive, cruel and dishonest, we must live up to our promises, do what we say we will and act in such a way that the world benefits.

5   Correct vocation. To harm others by one's occupation or to take advantage of them is destructive. In our day, with so much harm being done to the environment by careless, heedless ways of living, it's hard to say what the correct vocation is, but each person should consider theirs carefully.

6   Correct effort. This is the energy and will to get on with one's work, not to be deflected more than one can help, and to be constant in one's determination to tread the path.

7   Correct alertness. The goal of this step is to cultivate proper attention and awareness so that one is in control of one's actions. It is capturing the attention and bringing it to bear on what is happening now, at this moment, without memories and anticipations to cloud the scene, so that one sees things as they really are in a sharp and clear consciousness.

8   Correct concentration. This is practised during meditation. It is a form of mind training in which thought is persuaded to die down altogether and a tranquil one-pointedness is encouraged, which is usually accompanied by feelings of joy and wellbeing. Then these feelings themselves are allowed to die away so that all that remains is a clear transcendent awareness.

These steps lead to insight into one's fundamental nature, said the Buddha, and they bring about four sublime states – benevolence, compassion, joyous sympathy and equanimity. 'Be not afraid of good actions, brethren. It is another name for happiness, for what is desired, beloved, dear and delightful – this word "good actions".'

> The eightfold path is the best of all paths, the four truths the best of all truths. Freedom from craving is the best state, and the one who has eyes to see is the best person.
>
> This is the noble path, the way which leads to freedom from delusion, to clarity.
>
> The one who sees this path and follows it comes to the end of sorrow.
>
> *The Dhammapada*: The Path, verses 273, 274, 275

The Buddhist scriptures contain hundreds of discourses said to have been given by the Buddha during his long teaching life, but nearly all of them are centred on one or other of the eight steps. His explanations are adapted to the capacity of his audience to understand them. This is because the steps themselves encompass the whole of human nature. They can be taken at any level and each one of them (they are not meant to be taken consecutively) can be the start of a truth-seeking life. The Buddha wanted to reach all people, not just the scholarly, and therefore his message was that there are certain actions, clearly outlined, which can be started now by anybody, from the lowest outcast to the greatest king.

Watchfulness is the path to life, and thoughtlessness the path to death. The watchful are alive, but the thoughtless are already like the dead.

Awake, and rejoice in watchfulness. Understand the wisdom of the enlightened . . .

By watching keenly and working hard the wise man may build himself an island which no flood can sweep away.

The Dhammapada: Watchfulness, verses 21, 22, 25

When the Buddha left the palace, he was determined to find a way of life with greater meaning than that followed by a spoilt young prince. But as the truth of the way came home to him, he also saw that the life of society was full of deep divisions. There were frequent wars between petty chiefs and rival clans. The caste system, which still exists today, was beginning to dominate society. The struggle to better oneself and to climb another rung in the ladder of opportunity was becoming increasingly difficult. Religious insight, which has always underpinned Indian life, was being choked by the Brahmins (the priestly caste) who taught the *Vedas* as authoritative texts to be obeyed, rather than as living truths to be explored. Rites and ceremonies had to be performed with strict correctness. Also (worse in the Buddha's eyes) some influential Brahmins were taking up cosmological systems (religion according to the stars) and showering contempt on anyone who disagreed with them. A miasma of discouraged fatalism had settled on the majority of Hindus who, believing in reincarnation, saw no hope of release from the eternal round of birth and death. Nothing vexed the Buddha more than the way in which the Brahmins had turned themselves into a privileged caste by keeping the most valuable teachings back from the people and holding them as secret, powerful possessions.

Men and women were being misled. Their poignant immediate needs were being ignored in favour of distant heavens, and they were not being shown a nearer fulfilment and a much more dependable source of happiness. Instead they were becoming caught up in blind adherence to tradition, endless repetitive ritual and outlandish dogma. The Buddha saw it as his task to clear away these binding entanglements and to enable people to break through to a more lasting solution to their problems and in this way to bring to India a method of living which was full of freedom and love. As Martin Luther opposed the hypocrisy of the priests who sold indulgences, so the Buddha broke the hold of the Brahmins by preaching a religion which was devoid of authority and which relied on the individual to tread the path by his own power. It was a religion in which there were no secrets and no speculation.

> Celebrate the one who has woken. Celebrate the fire of his sacrifice and learn from him the way.
>
> Neither matted hair, nor noble birth nor caste makes a wise man, but the truth and integrity with which he is blessed.
>
> *The Dhammapada*: The Enlightened, verses 392, 393

His dedication to the good of all brought him the trust of many people. Beggars could go to him, knowing that they would be welcomed with unfailing and undiscriminating friendliness, for the Buddha discarded the caste system completely. At the same time he was trusted by kings and rulers and asked to adjudicate in disputes. It is claimed by historians that he started a whole civilization of wisdom and compassion and it is certainly true that Buddhism, throughout its history and its spread around the world, has produced no religious wars and has founded some very good societies.

The Buddha believed that suppressing crime through punishment was not the right solution. He suggested, instead, that if the economic condition of the people was improved, this would help bring crime down to manageable proportions. He wanted grain and other agricultural facilities to be given to farmers; capital should be available for traders to start up businesses; adequate wages should be paid to all those employed. When people have security of basic income and opportunities for earning more, they will be more contented, have less fear and anxiety, and the country would become a peaceful one.

There are four ways, he told his lay followers, in which a householder can find happiness. First, he should be skilled and energetic in whatever job he has; second, he should look after the money he earns and not squander it; third, he should have good friends who are 'faithful, virtuous, liberal and intelligent' and who will help him in his psychological life; and fourth, he should practise charity and generosity.

Wisdom and compassion came to be the two

qualities most associated with Buddhism. This was perhaps because the Buddha himself combined the two in a way that is rare among people. The many stories about him show him to be a man who was deeply sympathetic and responsive to any situation, endlessly patient, and strong and gentle and with unfailing goodwill. If the questioner was sincere, he was always answered readily. His followers regarded him with a wondering, eager devotion. But he was also a true thinker, an unexcelled philosopher. He was a giant in human history with his outstanding ability for analytic understanding. He investigated all the religious thought of his day, accepting what seemed to him clearly of value and rejecting or radically revising that which did not lead to the truth.

Because of these characteristics, Buddhism is the only world religion to be openly based on a systematic and rational analysis of life as it is lived, its problems and their solutions. The Buddha has been called a philosophic genius and a true lover of humankind rolled into one vigorous and radiant personality.

The content of *The Dhammapada* represents the essence of the Buddha's teaching. During his long life he delivered many sermons and gave much advice; often of an unconventional kind. For instance, when a girl came to him carrying her dead baby because she could not bear to put it down he did not make the obvious suggestion that she should part with the body. Instead he told her to get him some mustard seeds (the most common of all spices), and that she must get them from a household where there had never in living memory been a death. Eagerly she tried to find some, but wherever she went she found that somebody had died and people had grieved. She realized then that death is not unique and that to grieve is natural and she was able to put her baby down and allow it to be cremated.

The realization was hers, and the Buddha only led her to it. In the same way, he was convinced that people must reach decisions themselves, and that all he could do was make clear to them what those decisions entailed. He detested blind belief; and the idea that people would follow what he said just because it was he who said it was anathema to him.

Consequently, when he became deeply concerned about morality, he made clear what the basis of morality is and showed that people should always have a choice. India had its full share of crime and violence at that time, and the Buddha saw that this kind of life leads to great unhappiness. Therefore he advised all those who came to him inquiring about the Buddhist way of life to examine their own behaviour. It was no good, he said, trying to go straight to the inner life, to the liberation of the mind, before the outer life was put in order.

He particularly wanted followers to work out for themselves when they were pursuing an unwise course, for he wanted the morality he spoke about to be a natural morality. It should be based on an individual's understanding, through experience, of the results of actions. Then the choice to follow this way rather than that would be a conscious and informed one. Neither obedience, nor fear, nor love are involved here, only an understanding based on experimentation and careful choice. There is no 'thou shalt' or 'shalt not', but the follower is invited to take upon himself certain rules of training which he may find helpful in bringing about the confidence and self-reliance that lead to a sense of balance and harmony.

The moral teaching which the Buddha formulated is known as the 'five precepts'.

1   The follower undertakes to refrain from harming living beings.

2   The follower undertakes to refrain from taking what is not given.

3   The follower undertakes to refrain from a misuse of the senses.

4   The follower undertakes to refrain from wrong speech.

5   The follower undertakes to refrain from taking substances likely to cloud the mind.

The central teaching practice is a system of meditation designed to clarify the mind in such a way that knowledge and insight arise without impediment. As an essential preparation, therefore, these five precepts help the follower not to do anything which would impair the clarity of his mental vision or which would give him a false sense of euphoria, or encourage him to see things as other than they really are.

The Buddha saw clearly that when the mind is preoccupied with the results of bad actions, there can be no liberation. So he impressed on his disciples the fact that bad actions lead to guilt, worry and unhappiness, while good ones lead to a peaceful mind and happiness. This is made clear in the very first stanzas of the *The Dhammapada*.

> All that we are is the result of our thoughts; it is founded on our thoughts and made up of our thoughts. With our thoughts we make the world. If a man speaks or acts with a harmful thought, trouble follows him, as the wheel follows the ox that draws the cart.
>
> All that we are is the result of our thoughts, it is founded on our thoughts and made up of our thoughts. With our thoughts we make the world. If a man speaks or acts with a harmonious thought, happiness follows him as his own shadow, never leaving him.
>
> *The Dhammapada*: The Choice, verses 1 and 2

With the outer life in order, the inner life can begin. This, in Buddhism, centres around meditation. The Buddha continued to meditate for three hours every day throughout his life. During the rainy season, when it was impossible for his monks to walk freely, he initiated a three-month retreat period when they would gather together in various shelters and spend most of their time in meditation.

Throughout the course of Buddhist history, a number of ways of meditation have developed, starting with a very simple watching of the breath, and moving on to more advanced areas of concentration.

The Dhammapada contains several references to meditation. The most direct one is this:

Meditate, do your work attentively, and live in
quietness. The one who lives thus is indeed a sage.

The sun shines by day and the sage in his
wisdom shines. The moon shines by night and the
sage shines in meditation. But day and night, the
enlightened shine in radiance of the spirit.

The Dhammapada: The Enlightened, verses 386, 387

In order to meditate you should sit comfortably,
but as straight as possible so that the breathing is
not restricted, with your hands resting in the lap
and your eyes half closed. When you have arranged
yourself, you should start observing your breath.
The breath is something we take for granted, and we
only think about it when there is some problem
with it. Certainly, we don't usually observe it, but in
this basic practice of meditation, that is exactly what
we do. So you breathe in and out just as usual,
without any particular effort or change. But instead
of then letting the mind wander, you try to stay
aware of the breathing by simply watching it and
observing it. Breathing normally and naturally, you
may find that sometimes you take deep breaths and
sometimes not, but this does not matter at all. The
only thing to remember is that when you take a
deep breath you should be aware that it is a deep
breath. Your attention should be so focused on
your breathing that you become fully conscious of
its movements and changes.

At first you will find it very hard to keep your
mind on the breathing. Endlessly the mind runs
away, and you think of all sorts of things. You hear
sounds and at once identify them. Your mind is

constantly distracted, and you may feel the whole effort is a waste of time. But if you continue to practise this breathing for five or ten minutes at a time, once or twice a day, you will find that the whole thing changes. Your thoughts settle down and the outside world loses its power to attract them. Instead there is a growing sense of timelessness, a feeling that the busy chattering mind can be put down and some other dimension of existence can, for the first time, be apprehended.

This breathing practice, which is the simplest and easiest of all, is one which is practised throughout Buddhism and is meant to develop concentration, leading to a deep understanding and insight into the nature of things. But there are other immediate benefits. One's breathing is totally dependable; one can always rely on the fact that one is breathing and some of the calm and concentration developed will carry over into all one's affairs. Problems will not necessarily be solved, but the meditator will feel more capable of dealing with them. As a central point of tranquility grows, there will be a better sense of proportion and perspective on life. Hopes, fears and disappointments will still affect one, but their impact will be lessened by one's inner calm and so one will be much less likely to rush hastily into the wrong action. In fact, the breath can become a lifeline at any moment of stress, returning one to an inner sense of safety and calm.

> From meditation comes wisdom, and from lack of
> it wisdom decays. These are the two roads. Choose
> your one and let wisdom increase.
>
> *The Dhammapada*: The Path, verse 282

    e, and in your wisdom realize Nirvana, the
  * * happiness . . .

    y awake. Watch and reflect. Work with care-
    tention. In this way you will find the light
    n yourself . . .

    *W*atchful among the thoughtless, awake among
    sleepers, the meditating man advances like a
    er, without hindrance.

    he Dhammapada: Watchfulness, verses 23, 27, 29

*T*he Buddha was emphatic that it is the sense of
being a separate person that is at the root of unhappiness, especially when we believe that there can be
no other state. 'In the sitting, let there just be the
sitting,' he advised. 'In the standing, just the standing; in the walking, just the walking and in the
thinking just the thought.' In this way of behaviour,
the feeling of being a demanding person is lessened.
Buddhists also practise a similar exercise in which
they try to eliminate the word 'I' from their
thoughts. Thus, if you are going to open a door,
instead of thinking to yourself, 'I will open the door'
you think, 'There is an opening of the door'. In a
similar way, there is an eating of a meal, reading of
a book, or talking to a friend. This exercise can be
surprisingly effective and very calming.

    To try and forget the self can be bewildering to
Western followers who are used to the promotion
of the ego. What can replace the sense of self? Some
sort of amorphous nothingness? Not so, said the
Buddha. As the sense of self diminishes, there is discovered 'the wondrous bright True Mind'. He
urged his followers to examine their senses and to
understand that all they perceived could be

returned to its origin in the world. 'There is
without the sun and since light comes from t.
it can be returned to it. Darkness can be returi.
the waning moon, clearness to open doors
windows, obstruction to walls and houses, confus
externals to unconsciousness and clear perception
to the awakened state. Nothing in the world goes
beyond these conditions. But when the essence of
your Perception confronts these states, where can
it be returned to? Although these states such as
light, darkness and so on differ from one another,
your seeing does not differ, your seeing remains
unchanged.

'All states that can be returned to external causes
are obviously not *you*, but that which cannot be
returned to anywhere, if it is not *you*, what is it?
Therefore, you should know that your mind is
fundamentally wonderful, bright and pure and that
because of your delusion and ignorance, you have
missed it and so are caught, sinking and floating in
the sea of endless becoming.'

So his teaching was that we are creatures who
are fundamentally wonderful in mind, but deeply
misled by our cravings. In *The Dhammapada* this is
made clear.

Do not live thoughtlessly, in distraction and with
deluded aims, outside the universal Law.
Rouse yourself and follow the enlightened way
through the world with energy and joy.
Follow the path of enlightenment with happiness through this world and beyond.
See the world as a bubble, a mirage. Be
non-attached and death cannot touch you.

Look at this glittering world like a royal carriage; the foolish are enraptured with it but the wise do not cling to it.

The Dhammapada: The World, verses 167, 168, 169, 170, 171

It was said at the beginning of this introduction that *The Dhammapada* contains the essence of the Buddha's teaching. As well as the aspects of the teaching so far discussed, it gives advice on subjects such as mischief, violence, on what to do with yourself ('Love yourself and watch – today, tomorrow, always'), on the world, on anger, on justice, and on being a seeker, as well as on other topics. It is an invaluable source of inspiration to all people, whether Buddhist or not.

When the Buddha came to the end of his life, he knew that there would be a tendency among his followers both to see him as divine and to follow his teachings as dogma. He sincerely believed that this would be utterly wrong and he emphasized on his deathbed his great belief that everyone should find the truth for themselves. 'Be a lamp unto yourself,' he said. 'Rely on yourself and do not rely on external help. Hold fast to the truth as a lamp. Seek your salvation in the truth alone.

'Those who, either now or after I am dead, shall be a lamp unto themselves, relying on themselves only and not relying upon external help, holding fast to the truth as their lamp – it is they among my followers who shall reach the very topmost height.'

On the point of death, you have not prepared for the last journey.

Let a man be a lamp to himself and learn wisdom. When he is free from delusion, he will go beyond birth and death.

The Dhammapada: Impurity, verses 235, 236

The Buddha believed that it is possible for anyone to transcend the ego and to find higher states of awareness. He also believed that it is not possible to live a really happy life without genuine transcendence and spirituality. Such a belief as his had nothing to do with the myths that are part of most religions but is concerned with actual contemplative consciousness. Such a consciousness is sublime, but it is not automatic. One of the first things one finds out is that in order to be transformed one has to grow – and growth and transformation can hurt because they mean dying to the old and being born into the new. Many people prefer a more traditional religious path in which they are told what to believe and, although exhorted to be moral, are not expected to make great spiritual efforts. To this attitude, Buddhism would only point out that there is great joy in awakening.

It is hard to be born as a human being, and hard to live the life of one. It is even harder to hear of the path; and harder still to awake, to rise and to follow.

Yet the teaching of the Buddha is simple. 'Cease to do evil, learn to do good, and purify your mind.'

Patience is the best training and freedom is at

the end of the path. Patience and long-suffering mean that the follower will do no harm to another.

The Dhammapada: The Awakened One, verses
182, 183, 184

Spiritual thinkers have pointed out that during the first half of one's life one develops from pre-rational to rational, from a pre-ego stage to an egoic mode of awareness, from pre-personal to personal. Proper human growth depends on the healthy development of the personality, of an integrated mature ego. As with any abnormal or pathological condition, there is always trouble where the ego is malformed or underdeveloped.

When it seems as though the way is lost, however, is when, out of self-delusion, we cling to a construct, the ego, which we ourselves keep alive and foster; and in our clinging we lose our natural harmony with life and our understanding of its meaning and purpose.

The Buddha wanted to show that this need not happen, that once the personality is formed, the next stage of growth beyond the ego can begin. This is the evolution from egoic to trans-egoic. As present day thinker, Ken Wilber, says, it is the development from rational to trans-rational, from personal to trans-personal, from individual to spiritual.

In the West, particularly within the last fifty years, we have made much of the stages of growth that lead up to the mature personality, pointing out the traumas and neuroses that occur if this growth is disrupted or deformed. But only the mystics have ever attempted to say that there are stages of growth beyond the ego, and many Western psychologists would deny this vehemently.

The East, in contrast, has found almost nothing to say about the early stages from pre-ego to ego. Eastern religion, particularly Buddhism, begins with the mature ego and is concerned only to teach the transformational processes of spiritual stages leading towards the trans-egoic and the trans-personal.

Thus Buddhism is a path that leads away from infantile dependence (on gods and goddesses, with all their human characteristics) to adult integration and independence.

> Who else but the self can be master of the self? With self well controlled, there is no other master.
>
> By oneself evil is done; by oneself one suffers. By oneself good is done, by oneself one is purified. Purity and impurity belong to oneself. No one can purify another.
>
> Your work is to find out what your work should be and not to neglect it for another's. Clearly discover your work and attend to it with all your heart.
>
> *The Dhammapada*: Self, verses 160, 165, 166

The Buddha occasionally spoke of different states of existence – the world of spirits, blissful or tormented, of unhappy ghosts, the world of animals and the world of humans. His followers believed he was able to comprehend various levels of existence. Yet repeatedly he taught that it is only on this human plane that the path to liberation can be undertaken. Other planes, such as those experienced under mind-changing drugs, can be blissful, but they don't produce the right circumstances in which to find enlightenment. All our conflicts and confusions, our struggles for security and riches, the suffering that characterizes human life, all this is the very material from which liberation arises. We have to work out our salvation in the midst of trouble with the neighbours and atmospheric pollution and the growing crime rate.

To do this, we have to put away our childish clinging and dependence, our grasping at life, and recognize instead that life utterly defeats our efforts to control it, that all our striving for permanence is a hand held up to stop the wind. If we can but see that to lose one's life is to find it, our frustration and despair will turn into joy and creative power, and our actions will become free of self-frustration and the anxiety inherent in trying to control the world. Then, at last, we may see that this life is our greatest gift and this superb and wonderful organism which is ourselves is our one means of transformation. The Buddha said:

'In this very body, six feet in length, with its sense-impressions and its thoughts and ideas, I do declare to you is the world, and the origin of the world, and the ceasing of the world, and likewise the Way that leads to that ceasing.'

The Dhammapada

1 The Choice

v1   All that we are is the result of our thoughts; it is founded on our thoughts and made up of our thoughts. With our thoughts we make the world. If a man speaks or acts with a harmful thought, trouble follows him as the wheel follows the ox that draws the cart.

v2   All that we are is the result of our thoughts; it is founded on our thoughts and made up of our thoughts. With our thoughts we make the world. If a man speaks or acts with a harmonious thought happiness follows him as his own shadow, never leaving him.

v3   'He beat me, he robbed me. Look at how he abused and injured me.' Live with those thoughts and you will never stop hating.

v4   'He beat me, he robbed me. Look at how he abused and injured me.' Abandon such thoughts and your hatred and your suffering will cease.

v5   Hating can never overcome hatred. Only love can bring the end of hating. This is the eternal law.

v6　You too will die one day, as everyone must. When you know this, your hatred is stilled.

v7　As the wind blows down a shallow-rooted tree, so temptation overcomes the one who longs for pleasure, who is excessive, idle and weak.

v8　As the wind can never blow down a mountain, so temptation does not overcome the one who puts away pleasure, who is moderate, faithful and strong.

v9　The one who is careless, who does not bother with moderation or truth, is not worthy to be a follower of the path.

v10　But the one who minds about his conduct, who has purified himself and is calm, moderate and truthful, he is worthy to be a follower of the path.

v11　Those who mistake the appearance for the reality, the shadow for the substance and the true for the false, fill themselves with desires.

v12　But when you see the substance as the substance and the shadow as the shadow you see Reality directly, and follow your true nature.

v13　An easily swayed mind has no strength. Like the rain pouring into a badly roofed house, desires flood the person.

v14 Craving cannot break into a strong and understanding mind, just as the rain does not break into a well-thatched house.

v15 Whoever does harm will suffer in this world and the next. They will suffer when they see the results of their mischief.

v16 But the good will rejoice here and rejoice there when they see the good things they have done. They delight and rejoice in their own good deeds. They are happy to follow the path onwards.

v17 The one who does harm suffers both in this world and the next. He suffers when he thinks about what he has done and he suffers more when he wonders what will happen to him.

v18 The one who does good is happy both in this world and the next. He is happy when he thinks about the good he has done and happier still when he contemplates the path ahead.

v19 The one who talks of the path but never walks it himself is like a cowman counting the cattle of others but who has none of his own.

v20 All the holy words you read and all the holy words you speak are as nothing if you do not act upon them. Even if you read little and say little but live the right way, forsaking craving, hatred and delusion, you will know truth and find calmness and will show others the path.

2 Watchfulness

v21 Watchfulness is the path to life, and thoughtlessness the path to death. The watchful are alive, but the thoughtless are already like the dead.

v22 Awake, and rejoice in watchfulness. Understand the wisdom of the enlightened.

v23 Meditate, and in your wisdom realize Nirvana, the highest happiness.

v24 A kindly person who is energetic for good will be looked upon well by everybody.

v25 By watching keenly and working hard the wise man may build himself an island which no flood can sweep away.

v26 The thoughtless man does not care, but the attentive man looks on wakefulness as his greatest treasure.

v27 Stay awake. Watch and reflect. Work with careful attention. In this way you will find the light within yourself.

v28 He is one who has overcome craving and exchanged the folly of delusion for the stronghold of wisdom. He looks down upon the suffering and the ignorant, on the delinquent and the foolish, and sees that they live close to the ground.

v29 Watchful among the thoughtless, awake among the sleepers, the meditating man advances like a racer, without hindrance.

v30 By attentiveness Indra became chief of the gods. He found the joy of attention and the foolishness of sleep.

v31 The seeker who guards his thoughts and fears the wilfulness of his mind, burns through the bonds which tie him with the fire of his attentiveness.

v32 The seeker who guards his thoughts and fears his own delusions can never fall. He now knows the way to bliss.

3 The Mind

v33 As the bowman makes straight his arrows, so the wise man straightens his unsteady mind.

v34 This mind is like a fish out of water which thrashes and throws itself about, when thoughts try to shake off their cravings.

v35 Such a wandering mind is weak and unsteady, attracted here, there and everywhere. How good it is to control it and know the happiness of freedom.

v36 And yet how unruly still, how subtle the delusion of the thoughts. To quiet them and master them is the true way to happiness.

v37 Putting a bridle on the wandering mind, single-mindedly the seeker halts his thoughts. He ends their darting waywardness and finds peace.

v38 A troubled mind, however, does not see the way. If a man is ignorant and filled with doubt, he can never find the true path.

v39 But a concentrated mind, untroubled and calm, no longer struggling to judge between right and wrong but beyond judgements has no fear, for it understands.

v40 He knows that the body is as fragile as a jar. By making the mind as firm as a fortress, wisdom and understanding will fight for him in every trial, guarding all that has been won.

v41 For soon the body will be cast aside and what will be its consciousness then? It will lie on the ground like a useless log of wood, without knowledge or feeling.

v42 Whatever an enemy may do, he cannot harm you as much as your own wrongly directed thoughts.

v43 But once you understand, no one – neither your father nor mother – can do as much good to you as your own well-directed thoughts.

4 Flowers

v44   Who will transcend this world? Who will transcend the realm of the dead, and heaven too with all its gods? Who will find the true and shining way of the path?

v45   You will. Even as the gatherer of flowers discovers the finest and the rarest, so will you gather the teachings and transcend this world.

v46   When you know that the body is merely the foam on the crest of a wave, unreal as a mirage, you will break the flowery arrows of craving. Unseen, you will escape the King of Death and travel onwards.

v47   The flowers of pleasure tempt the thoughtless man. But when he gathers them, death overtakes him as a flood sweeps away a sleeping village.

v48   While such a thoughtless man is gathering the flowers of pleasure, he is overtaken by death before he can ever be satisfied.

v49   When the bee collects honey it does not spoil the beauty or scent of the flower. So let the sage settle in himself and wander as he wills.

v50 Do not remark on the faults of others, but see what you yourself have done or left undone. Then overlook the faults of others.

v51 Like beautiful flowers that have colour but no scent are the eloquent but empty sayings of the man who does not act according to his words.

v52 Like beautiful flowers full of colour and fragrance are the fruitful sayings of the man who acts according to his words.

v53 As many garlands as can be made from a pile of flowers, so make as many good deeds from your life.

v54 The scent of sandalwood, lilies and jasmine cannot travel against the wind, but the fragrance of good works travels in all directions, even to the ends of the earth.

v55 How much sweeter than the scent of sandalwood or jasmine is the fragrance of good deeds!

v56 The scent of lotus, lily and jasmine carries only a little way, but the fragrance of goodness rises to heaven.

v57 Craving never blocks the path of those who live upright lives. Their wisdom sets them free.

v58 How brightly the lotus grows in the rubbish by the wayside. Its sweet scent lightens the heart.

v59 So you, the awakened, will shine in the darkness around you, spreading the sweet scent of your wisdom.

5 The Fool

v60   Long is the night to the watcher; long is the road to the weary traveller; long is the path to the foolish who stray through many lives searching for it.

v61   If the traveller cannot find a wise friend to go with him, let him go on alone. It is better than having a fool for company.

v62   The fool thinks anxiously, 'These children and this wealth is mine.' But he is not even master of himself, much less of children and possessions.

v63   The fool who knows he is a fool is wise so far, but the fool who thinks he is wise is truly a fool.

v64   Though a fool knows a wise man all his life, he will understand the truth as little as the spoon savours the soup.

v65   But when a thoughtful man knows a wise man, even for a little while, he will understand, as the tongue knows the taste of the soup.

v66   Fools are their own greatest enemies for the trouble they make bears bitter fruit.

v67 Ill deeds bring great remorse. Their fruit is reaped in sorrow.

v68 Do only what you will not regret and the fruit of your deeds will be reaped in joy.

v69 The fool thinks that the mischief he makes is as sweet as honey till it bears its fruit, and then he suffers.

v70 Though a man should fast and eat his food from the tip of a grass blade, yet he is still not worth the smallest part of those to whom the food is the way.

v71 Fresh milk suddenly curdles in the heat, but a bad deed pursues the fool slowly like a smouldering fire.

v72 The fool obtains knowledge but without wisdom it produces woe, it destroys his own happiness.

v73 He wants a high place in the world, recognition and fame so that all will look up to him.

v74 He thinks, 'May everyone praise me and obey me.' Those are his desires and his overwhelming pride.

v75 This way leads to wealth and worldly success. The other way leads to the end of the path. The follower of the Buddha, therefore, does not look for recognition and the praise of men but goes the way of the awakened and sets himself free.

6 The Wise Man

v76 Look upon the wise man who shows you where you are mistaken as a revealer of treasures. It is good to know such a man.

v77 Let him advise others, and prevent wrong-doing. The good will love him and only the bad will hate him.

v78 The wise man will not keep bad company but will seek the fellowship of those who love truth.

v79 The wise man follows the way of the awakened. He lives happily, with his mind at ease.

v80 Irrigators guide water; fletchers straighten arrows; carpenters turn wood; wise people shape themselves.

v81 As a rock remains unmoved by storm, so the wise remain unmoved by praise or blame.

v82 Hearing the truth, the wise become like a calm, unruffled lake.

v83 The wise walk on, clinging to nothing. They are neither elated by happiness nor cast down by sorrow.

v84 Neither for himself nor for others will the wise man crave family or wealth. He will not wish to gain by others' loss.

v85 Few cross the river to the further shore. The rest run up and down this side of the torrent.

v86 But those who pursue the truth will reach the further shore, and pass through the realm of death, which is so hard to cross.

v87 Leaving the way of darkness, the wise man will follow the way of light. Giving up his security he will enter into solitude, knowing the road to be hard.

v88 Putting away desire and freeing himself from possessions, the wise man will rid himself of all dark thoughts.

v89 With his mind full of regard for the truth; with energy, concentration and calmness; clinging to nothing and overcoming all dark thoughts, he is awakened and enters Nirvana in this world.

7 The Sage

v90 There is freedom from desire and sorrow at the end of the way. The awakened man is free from all fetters and goes beyond life and death.

v91 Like a swan that rises from the lake, with his thoughts at peace he moves onward, never looking back.

v92 He who understands the unreality of all things, and who has laid up no store, his track is unseen, like that of birds in the air.

v93 Like a bird in the air he takes an invisible course, wanting nothing, storing nothing, knowing the emptiness of all things.

v94 Even the gods must admire him who, like a charioteer, has brought his horses under control and has put away pride and craving.

v95 Tolerant like the earth, firm as a rock, and clear as a mountain pool, such a man is free from birth and death.

v96 Still and calm is he who has awakened. His mind is peaceful and his words and deeds reflect this.

v97 He is the greatest of men who is not credulous, knows the reality of Nirvana, has gone beyond birth and death and broken every bond.

v98 In village or forest, on the hills or in the plain, wherever the awakened ones live is delightful.

v99 Delightful are those forests where the worldly fail to find delight. There the awakened ones are joyful, wanting nothing.

8 The Thousands

v100 Better than a thousand meaningless words is one word of sense, which brings the hearer peace.

v101 Better than a thousand senseless verses is one which brings the hearer peace.

v102 Better than a thousand useless verses is one word of the truth which brings the hearer peace.

v103 Though one man conquer a thousand men in battle a thousand times, he who conquers himself is the greatest warrior.

v104 The conquest of oneself is better than the conquest of all others.

v105 Neither gods nor demons can turn this victory into a defeat.

v106 Though a man sacrifice a thousand pieces of money every month for a hundred years, one moment of reverence for the possessor of true knowledge is of more avail.

v107 Though a man should offer sacrifices for a hundred years, one moment of homage for he who is awake is of greater benefit.

v108 Whatever offering a man may make to gain merit, it is not worth a small part of reverence for a wise man.

v109 Revering such a man, even when he has grown old in his wisdom, will bring happiness and beauty and strength.

v110 Better than a hundred years of uncontrolled existence is one day of thoughtful and meditative life.

v111 Better than a hundred years of ignorance and folly is one day of wise and clear-sighted living.

v112 Better than a hundred years of idleness is one day spent with energy and determination.

v113 Better to understand for a single day the fleeting nature of things than to live for a hundred years without such understanding.

v114 Better one day with a vision of life beyond the Way than a hundred years of blindness to the truth.

v115 Better one day with a knowledge of the Way than a hundred years of ignorance.

9 Trouble

v116 Better to do good than harm, and better to do it at once. If a man hesitates and is slow to do good, he is easily seized by mischief.

v117 Turn away from wrong-doing and take no pleasure in it. Turn away from it again and again, for sorrow is its outcome.

v118 Do good, and do it again and again, and gladness and happiness will be the outcome.

v119 Even a wrongdoer is happy so long as his evil has not ripened, but when it bears its fruit he suffers.

v120 Even a good man suffers trouble while his good deed has not ripened, but when it bears fruit he is happy.

v121 Let no man think lightly of wrong-doing: 'It will not touch me.' Drop by drop is the pitcher filled, and little by little the fool becomes filled with folly.

v122 Do not belittle your own goodness: 'I have not deserved this.' Drop by drop the pitcher is filled and the wise man is filled with virtue.

v123 Let a man avoid wrong-doing, as a merchant with few friends and great wealth avoids a dangerous road, or as a man who wishes to live avoids poison.

v124 He who has no wound may touch poison with his hand, and it will not harm him. There is no harm for one who does no harm.

v125 Like dust thrown against the wind, trouble falls back upon the fool who harms the harmless.

v126 Some come to rebirth, others to states of heaven or hell; those who are free from the bonds that tie them realize Nirvana.

v127 Not in the sky, nor in the sea, nor in a cave in the mountains can a man escape from his harmful deeds.

v128 Not in the sky, nor in the sea, nor in a cave in the mountains can a man find a place where death cannot overcome him.

10 Punishment

v129 All men fear pain and death. Remembering that he is one of them, let a man neither strike nor kill.

v130 All men fear pain and death, all men love life. Remembering that he is one of them, let a man neither strike nor kill.

v131 He who injures or kills one who is seeking for happiness, will not find it for himself.

v132 He who does no harm to beings who long for happiness, will find it for himself.

v133 Let no man speak harshly to another, for he will answer in the same way. Angry speech brings trouble and blows in return.

v134 He who is silent like a gong which is broken, knows stillness. He reaches freedom, where there is no more striving.

v135 As a cowman drives his cattle to pasture, so old age and death drive all before them.

v136 The fool pays no heed, not knowing when he makes mischief, and he lights the fire that consumes him.

v137 Whoever harms the harmless and offends the inoffensive will come to one of these misfortunes.

v138 He will have cruel suffering, great loss, accident or injury, severe illness, madness . . .

v139 Trouble with authorities, a dreadful accusation, death of relations, or loss of wealth . . .

v140 Or fire will burn his house, and upon his death he will go into the darkness.

v141 Not nakedness, nor matted hair, nor fasting nor sleeping on the ground, neither rubbing the body with dust nor sitting like an ascetic can purify a man who has not solved his doubts.

v142 Even though richly clothed, he who is calm and controlled, who lives a good life and does no harm to others is a true seeker.

v143 Is there in this world a man so restrained that he gives no occasion for reproach, as a noble horse never deserves the whip?

v144 Like a well-trained horse when touched by the whip, let a man be active, let him throw off this load of misery by faith, goodness, meditation, understanding of the way, and wisdom.

v145 Irrigators guide water; fletchers straighten arrows, carpenters turn wood; wise men shape themselves.

11 Old Age

v146 The world is ablaze! Yet people laugh. They are clouded deep in darkness. Why do they not seek the light?

v147 Look at your body – frail and sickly, racked with pains – how can it last?

v148 Your body wastes away, is full of disease and feebleness, and then it dies. Death is the end of life.

v149 Behold these bleaching bones, scattered like empty husks in the autumn.

v150 This body is a framework of bones, with flesh and blood as the plaster. It is the home of pride and hypocrisy, old age and death.

v151 Just as the brilliant carriages of kings wear out, so does the body become old. But the teachings of the wise never grow old, they pass on for ever to the good.

v152 The man who has learnt little grows old like an ox; his flesh increases but not his knowledge.

v153 (Spoken by the Buddha when he became enlightened) 'Through countless weary lives I have sought the builder of this house and could not find him.

v154 'Now I have found you, O Builder, and never again shall you build this house. The rafters are snapped, the ridgepole is shattered. My mind has reached the end of craving and is free.'

v155 Old herons die by a lake where there is no fish. Those who have frittered away their life and have earned nothing, perish in the same way.

v156 As sad as a worn-out bow, they sigh for all the life they have squandered.

12 Self

v157 If a man is dear to himself he will guard himself carefully. For at least a part of the night he will keep watch.

v158 Let a wise man first go the right way himself, then teach others. So he will have no cause to grieve.

v159 If a man is himself controlled, he will be able to control others. When he comes to know himself, he will be able to teach others.

v160 Who else but the self can be master of the self? With self well controlled there is no other master.

v161 The harm he does crushes the fool, even as a diamond crushes a precious stone.

v162 Just as a creeper chokes a tree, so a man's harmful deeds will bring him as low as his enemy would wish him to be.

v163 It is easy to lose yourself in mischief. What is helpful and good is often hard to do.

v164 Like the fruit of the bamboo tree which is its destruction, the senseless man who scorns the teachings of the awakened and follows false advice, bears the fruit of his own destruction.

v165 By oneself evil is done; by oneself one suffers. By oneself good is done; by oneself one is purified. Purity and impurity belong to oneself. No one can purify another.

v166 Your work is to find out what your work should be and not to neglect it for another's. Clearly discover your work and attend to it with all your heart.

13 The World

v167 Do not live thoughtlessly, in distraction and with deluded aims, outside the universal Law.

v168 Rouse yourself and follow the enlightened way through the world with energy and joy.

v169 Follow the path of enlightenment with happiness through this world and beyond.

v170 See the world as a bubble, a mirage. Be non-attached and death cannot touch you.

v171 Look at this glittering world, it is like a royal carriage. The foolish are taken up by it, but the wise do not cling to it.

v172 The moon comes out from behind the clouds and brightens up the world. So too the man who overcomes his ignorance shines forth.

v173 Like the moon coming out from behind the clouds, the man who sees his past mistakes and turns to good deeds, shines forth.

v174 The world is dark and only a few can see; only a few soar upwards like birds escaping from the fowler's net.

v175 Swans rise and fly through the air. How magical they are! So do the resolute conquer the armies of delusion and rise above the world.

v176 If you scorn the universal Law and scoff at the life to come, there is no end to your foolish mischief.

v177 The miser can never enter heaven and the fool scorns generosity. But the wise man finds joy in giving and enters heaven in this world.

v178 But better than all the happiness on earth or in heaven, greater than dominion over all the worlds, is the joy of the first step on the Noble Path.

14 The Awakened One

v179 He who has finally conquered, whose view is boundless, by what path can he be led astray?

v180 He whose view is boundless, and who is free from all craving, the Trackless One, by what path can he be led astray?

v181 Even the gods envy him who is enlightened and is given to meditation, who is free from craving.

v182 It is hard to be born as a human being, and hard to live the life of one. It is even harder to hear of the path; and harder still to awake, to rise and to follow.

v183 Yet the teaching of the Buddha is simple: 'Cease to do evil, learn to do good. And purify your mind.'

v184 Patience is the best training and freedom is at the end of the path. Patience and long-suffering means that the follower will do no harm to another.

v185 'Hurt none by word or deed. Be moderate in your eating. Live in inner solitude. And seek the deepest consciousness.' This is the teaching of the Buddha.

v186 Even a shower of gold would not satisfy the craving of lust. He is wise who knows that sensual pleasures are short and leave lasting dissatisfaction.

v187 Even heavenly pleasures are not lasting. The follower of the Buddha delights only in awakening.

v188 Driven by fear, a man may hide in one refuge after another. He may look for shelter on mountains or in forests, among sacred places or in shrines.

v189 But these are not safe refuges, for a man is not delivered from suffering in them.

v190 He who takes refuge in the Way and journeys with those who follow it, clearly sees the four great truths.

v191 Suffering, the cause of suffering, the ceasing of suffering and the eightfold path that leads to the end of suffering.

v192 Then at last he finds safety. He is delivered from suffering and is free.

v193 The awakened are few and are not easy to find. Happy is the family in which such a sage is born.

v194 Happy is the birth of the awakened one, happy his teaching of the path and happy are those who accompany him.

v195 Whoever reveres the man who is awake and those who follow him, that one will be free from craving and free from fear and will have crossed the river of sorrow.

v196 Whoever reveres the awakened one and the noble path, will live in measureless serenity and peace.

15 Happiness

v197 Live happily, without hating even those who hate you. Be free from hatred among those who hate.

v198 Live happily, in health, even among those who are sick.

v199 Live happily, free from greed among the greedy.

v200 Live happily, though you have no possessions. Be like the gods, feeding on love.

v201 Victory for one sows the seeds of hatred in another, for the loser is unhappy. Be calm and give up both victory and defeat.

v202 There is no fire like greed and no crime like hatred. There is no sorrow like being bound to this world; there is no happiness like freedom.

v203 Hunger is the greatest ill and this body the greatest source of sorrow; when one knows this Nirvana becomes the highest happiness.

v204 Health is the greatest of blessings, contentment the best riches, trust is the best of relationships; Nirvana is the highest happiness.

v205 Having tasted the sweetness of inner solitude and calmness, he who lives by the Law is free from fear and suffering.

v206 It is joy to see the awakened ones and to live with them is happiness.

v207 To travel with fools makes the journey long and hard and is as painful as travelling with an enemy. But the company of the wise is as pleasant as meeting with friends.

v208 Follow the wise, the intelligent and the awakened. Follow them as the moon follows the path of the stars.

16 Pleasure

v209 He who gives himself entirely to sensual pleasures and does not meditate, gives up the real for the pleasant. He comes to envy the man who pursues wisdom.

v210 Do not cling to the pleasant, much less to the unpleasant. Losing that which you love brings suffering; harbouring the pain of your loss brings more pain.

v211 Cling to nothing, for its loss is pain. Free yourself from attachment to the loved and the hated and you will loose the bonds which tie you.

v212 He who has overcome craving for what he loves is free from fear and grief.

v213 Clinging to the loved causes fear and brings sorrow, but he who has overcome this clinging is free.

v214 Clinging to sensual pleasures brings fear and sorrow, but by overcoming this clinging a man is free.

v215 From love of constant change and variety is born fear and sorrow. He who knows this is free from both.

v216 From craving is born fear and sorrow. He is free from craving who has no fear and no sorrow.

v217 The good man who speaks the truth and lives it is respected wherever he goes.

v218 The one whose mind is enlightened and free from craving and who strives for Nirvana, is called 'He who has crossed the stream.'

v219 Just as the man returned home from a journey is met by his relatives and friends . . .

v220 So the man of good deeds will be welcomed in his new life by those good deeds.

17 Anger

v221 Overcome anger and pride and all that binds you.
He who does not cling to his name and his status
and who possesses nothing will not be destroyed by
his sorrow.

v222 He who curbs his anger is like a charioteer control-
ling an unruly horse. Others merely hold the reins.

v223 Overcome anger with kindness, evil with goodness,
meanness with generosity and lying with truth.

v224 Let a man be truthful and calm, and give to those
who are in want. By these three means he will
perfect himself.

v225 The wise are free from hatred and are the con-
trollers of their minds. They will approach Nirvana
and go beyond sorrow.

v226 Those who meditate and are watchful day and night
will overcome their harmful thoughts and approach
Nirvana.

v227 This is an old saying: The man who is silent is
blamed; he who talks too much is blamed; he who
says little is blamed. Whatever he does, they blame
him.

v228 People always give praise or blame. They always have and they always will.

v229 He who is praised by the wise and lives a good life,

v230 Who would dare blame such man, who is like a coin of purest gold?

v231 Beware of anger in your body. Control your body and your anger will be overcome.

v232 Beware of anger in your speech. Control your speech and your anger will be overcome.

v233 Beware of anger in your mind. Guard your mind carefully and overcome your anger with gentleness.

v234 The wise man has control of body, tongue and mind. He is the true master.

18 Impurity

v235 On the point of death, you have not prepared for the last journey.

v236 Let a man be a lamp to himself and learn wisdom. When he is free from delusion, he will go beyond birth and death.

v237 Coming to the close of life you have made no provision for that last journey.

v238 Let a man make of himself an island and learn wisdom. When he is free from delusion, he will no longer be reborn.

v239 As a silversmith removes dust from silver, so the wise man rids himself gradually of all his impurities.

v240 As rust which springs from iron corrodes it, so the harm which men do destroys them.

v241 The sacred verses rust when they are not said, a house is destroyed when no one repairs it, beauty is marred through lazy neglect, the watchman is ruined by his carelessness.

v242 When a woman lacks loyalty and a man lacks generosity, there is impurity in this world and the next.

v243 The worst impurity of all is ignorance. Remove your ignorance and be pure.

v244 Life is easy for the shameless and bold man who is careless of others.

v245 But life is hard for the modest and thoughtful man who is active and considerate.

v246 If you destroy life, or take another man's wife, or lie and steal,

v247 And if you stupefy yourself with drink, you destroy your own roots.

v248 Do not make such suffering for yourself through your own greed and mischief.

v249 He who envies the food or gifts given to others will never know peace of mind for himself.

v250 But he who is not greedy has peace of mind by day and by night.

v251 There is no fire like hatred, no rushing river like craving, and no snare like illusion.

v252 How easy to see the faults of others, but how hard to see one's own. Men gossip about the faults of others, but hide their own as a cheat covers up a losing throw of the dice.

v253 He who always finds fault with others, will let his own faults multiply and is far from the end of his journey.

v254 No one whose thoughts are only of this world can be a follower of the awakened, for the world delights in craving and false values. The awakened are free from both.

v255 No one whose thoughts are only of this world can be a follower of the awakened. All things in this world are changing, but enlightenment remains for ever.

19 The Just

v256 Judge harshly and you will not be just. A wise man sees both sides and judges fairly.

v257 He who looks at all opinions equally, wisely, and with consideration is called upright.

v258 A man is not wise because he has much to say. The wise man is he who is patient, fearless and free from hatred.

v259 A man is not wise because he knows the scriptures. He may know little of the universal Law but if he lives it himself he is called honest.

v260 A man is not wise merely because his hair is grey. He may be old in years but he may also have grown old in vain.

v261 The mature person lives truthfully, in goodness and with calm control.

v262 A man is not upright because he speaks well or looks handsome.

v263 Only when he has rooted out selfishness and deceit, can he be called good.

v264 A man may put on the yellow robe of a monk but that does not make him virtuous. How can an undisciplined man who is still full of desires be virtuous?

v265 The truly virtuous man has rooted out his waywardness.

v266 A man is not a monk merely because he begs for food or follows all the rituals.

v267 He is a true follower who has gone beyond both good and evil and who lives in the awakened way.

v268 A man is not a sage merely because he is silent. He may well be hiding his dullness and ignorance.

v269 He who longs for good and rejects all evil, who meditates on this world and the next – he is the sage.

v270 A man is not noble if he injure any living creature. The noble man is gentle to all living creatures.

v271 It is not by learning, or by following ritual, nor is it by meditation alone or becoming a solitary seeker that one can find freedom.

v272 It is only through relying on nothing until you crave for nothing, that you will find the freedom of the awakened.

20 The Path

v273 The eightfold path is the best of all paths, the four truths the best of all truths. Freedom from craving is the best state, and the one who has eyes to see is the best person.

v274 This is the noble path, the way that leads to freedom from delusion, that leads to clarity.

v275 The one who sees this path and follows it comes to the end of sorrow.

v276 You yourself must make the effort, the awakened only point the way. Those who have entered the path and who meditate, free themselves from the bonds of illusion.

v277 Everything is changing. It arises and passes away. The one who realizes this is freed from sorrow. This is the shining path.

v278 To exist is to know suffering. Realize this and be free from suffering. This is the radiant path.

v279 There is no separate self to suffer. The one who understands this is free. This is the path of clarity.

v280 But if you are lazy and irresolute, idle when you should be energetic, such as you are will never find the path.

v281 Master your speech and train your thoughts. Never allow your body to act harmfully. Then you will enter the path.

v282 From meditation comes wisdom, and from lack of it wisdom decays. These are the two roads. Choose your one and let wisdom increase.

v283 Cut down the forest of craving – and not just one tree only since from the forest comes danger. Cut down all the trees and clear the undergrowth and be free.

v284 While a man lusts after a woman, his mind is bound as closely as a calf to its mother.

v285 Pluck out your love of yourself as the autumn flower is plucked, and enter the path of peace taught by the awakened.

v286 'Here I will spend the winter and summer.' So the fool makes plans, not even thinking of his death.

v287 But death will overtake him. Absorbed in his daily concerns, caring only for his children and his cattle, he will be carried off by death, even as a flood sweeps away a sleeping village.

v288 Neither relatives nor one's own family can give refuge when one is faced with death.

v289 Seeing that no one can help when one is overtaken by death, the wise will find the path that goes beyond death.

21 Forest Wisdom

v290 The wise will give up lesser pleasures to obtain joy.

v291 The one who finds pleasure in giving suffering to others will never be free from hatred.

v292 When you neglect your work and when, needlessly, you prefer to do wrong, your recklessness will lead to ever greater craving.

v293 The true master meditates and does no wrong. As he works, he watches, and his harmful thoughts grow fewer and fewer.

v294 Once, in his thoughts, he may have slain both his parents. He would have killed kings and all their subjects. But now, in his purity, he is free.

v295 Even though he would have killed both his father and mother and even great and worthy kings, yet he now goes free.

v296 The followers of the awakened are watchful and enlightened, as they remember the Buddha by day and by night.

v297 The followers of the awakened are watchful and enlightened, as they remember the universal Law by day and by night.

v298 The followers of the awakened are watchful and enlightened, as they remember the seekers of the path by day and by night.

v299 The followers of the awakened are watchful and enlightened, as they remember the mystery of the material world by day and by night.

v300 The followers of the awakened are watchful and enlightened, as they constantly seek happiness without violence.

v301 The followers of the awakened are always watchful and enlightened, as day and night they take joy in meditation.

v302 It is hard to leave the world for the life of a hermit; but just as hard to stay in the world and be a house-holder. To be with those who do not understand you is very hard. The road is long and painful for the unawakened.

v303 A person of confidence and goodness will be wel-comed wherever they go.

v304 The good shine from afar like the Himalayas in the sun. But the bad move in the darkness as hidden as arrows in the night.

v305 Sitting and sleeping and living alone within yourself, joyous and energetic, the silent forest will
delight you.

22 Torment

v306 The one who denies the truth goes into hell.

v307 Many monks who wear the yellow robe are not worthy of it and fall into hell.

v308 Better to swallow a ball of red-hot iron than to live a bad life at the expense of other people.

v309 Four things happen to a man who courts another's wife – he brings about trouble, his sleep is broken, he loses his reputation and he goes into hell.

v310 The hurried pleasure of the frightened man in the arms of the frightened woman brings not only a bad reputation, but punishment by the authorities. Let no man go after another's wife.

v311 Just as a blade of grass will cut the hand if clumsily grasped, so a life badly lived will destroy even a follower of the path.

v312 If you break your word through heedlessness, or live a good life only through fear of consequences, or act with lazy indifference, you will not find the path.

v313 Do what has to be done with a resolute heart. The lazy follower who hesitates merely scatters the dust about on the road.

v314 Better to leave a bad deed undone, knowing the suffering it causes, just as it is better to do a good deed which will not be regretted.

v315 Guard yourself like one in a fortified city. Do not relax your watchfulness for even a moment, lest you should fall into trouble.

v316 Those who are ashamed where there is nothing to be ashamed of, and those who have no shame when there should be shame, have wrong ideas which lead to their downfall.

v317 Those who are fearful when there is nothing to fear and those who travel carelessly through dangerous country – both hold wrong ideas which lead to their destruction.

v318 Those who imagine evil when there is no evil and those who see no evil where it exists, have false ideas which cause their own undoing.

v319 But those who observe evil as evil and good as good see correctly and reach a state of happiness.

23 The Elephant

v320 Just as the elephant endures the arrows of battle, so will I patiently bear hard words, for many in the world speak unkindly.

v321 The trained elephant is mounted by the king and led in procession. The self-controlled man who bears abuse patiently is the best among men.

v322 Camels and horses and elephants are excellent when trained, but more excellent is the man who has trained himself.

v323 A man does not reach Nirvana mounted on any animal, but by training himself.

v324 The elephant Dharapala is wild when he is in rut, and when he is captured he will not eat, but longs for the elephant forest.

v325 The fool who lolls lazily like a fat hog, feeding on temple food and spending his time eating and sleeping, will be reborn again and again.

v326 This mind of mine which used to wander just as it pleased, for as long as it liked, is now under my control, just as the elephant in rut is controlled by his driver.

v327 Be watchful and guard your thoughts, lifting your-self out of the bog of craving, hatred and delusion, as an elephant lifts himself out of the mud.

v328 If a traveller can walk gladly with a wise friend, he will overcome all his troubles.

v329 But if he cannot find a wise friend, then he should go on alone, like a king who has left his kingdom or an elephant which has left the elephant grove.

v330 It is better to live alone than have to live with a fool. Live alone, like the king elephant in the forest.

v331 Friends are pleasant in times of need, happiness is pleasant when shared with them, having done good deeds is pleasant at the hour of death, but happiest is the end of all suffering.

v332 To be a mother is a happy state and to be a father likewise. The life of the follower is happy and rever-ence for the awakened ones is joyful.

v333 Be good and you will be both happy and blissfully confident. Committing no error, you will obtain deep insight.

24 Craving

v334 Craving grows in the thoughtless like creepers in the jungle. Like monkeys looking for fruit in the trees the thoughtless bound from this life to that.

v335 If you are filled with craving, let your grief grow like the grass after rain.

v336 Suffering falls away from the one who overcomes craving, even as water drops from the lotus flower.

v337 Dig out the roots of craving as you would dig up the birana grass to get to the flesh root. Do not let evil crush you as a flood crushes the reeds.

v338 As a tree will sprout again when cut down if the roots are left, so craving will spring forth again unless completely overcome.

v339 The one in whom thirty-six streams lead towards sensual pleasures – eating and drinking and desire – will be destroyed by them, for his imagination is filled with wrong ideas.

v340 Streams flow in every direction and creepers force their way up and sprout. Seeing the creepers of craving, cut their roots with the sword of insight.

v341 Immersed in the stream of craving, how can you escape your rebirth?

v342 Bound by craving, like a hare in the net of the hunter, you circle round from life to life, always suffering.

v343 People are surrounded by craving like hares in the hunter's net. Let the one who is awake banish craving and be free from desire.

v344 You have come out of the pit and live your life in the clear. Are you foolish enough to rush back into the pit?

v345 The wise do not call manacles of iron or wood or rope as strong as the soft manacles of riches, wife and children. These are the strongest because although loose, they are harder to break.

v346 Those who have broken such bonds surrender the world and give up their sensual craving.

v347 Those who are still full of craving fall into their own stream, like a spider in the middle of its web. But the wise move out of the water, becoming free from craving.

v348 Giving up yesterday, today and tomorrow, the wise cross over to the farther shore, beyond birth and death.

v349 Craving grows like a thirst in the one who is torn by doubts, and is determined to find pleasure. Desire tightens the bonds.

v350 Overcome your doubts. Reflect and meditate. You will see that nothing binds you and temptation can be put down.

v351 When you are free from craving and have overcome doubt and fear you will have finished with the suffering of this life and will not return again.

v352 The one who is free from craving and deeply understands the teaching is known as a great sage. This is the last body of such a one.

v353 'I have overcome all things, understand all things, and am free from all things. I have surrendered everything and am free from all craving. Whom can I call Teacher?'

v354 The gift of the truth is greater than all other gifts; the taste of the truth is sweeter than all other; love of the truth goes beyond all other love; the end of craving is the end of suffering.

v355 The one who never looks for the other shore but seeks only the pleasures of the senses is destroyed. By seeking them, such a one is crushed by them.

v356 Weeds choke the field; craving poisons humanity. But a gift free from craving bears fine fruit.

v357 Weeds choke the field; hatred poisons humanity. A gift free from hatred bears fine fruit.

v358 Weeds choke the field; delusion poisons humanity. A gift free from delusion bears fine fruit.

v359 Weeds choke the field; humanity is poisoned by obsession with the body. A gift free from bodily obsession bears fine fruit.

25 The Seeker

v360 Learn mastery over your senses. Learn to control your eye and control your ear. In what you smell and taste, become the master.

v361 It is good to master your movements, to control your words and thoughts. The seeker who is in control in every way is joyful in freedom.

v362 When you are master of your limbs and of your concentration, you will delight in meditation and in solitude.

v363 It is good to listen to the seeker who guards his tongue and speaks wisely. Such a one is humble and does not exalt himself. He follows the universal Law in his daily life.

v364 The seeker who loves the truth and always reflects upon it, will always be sustained by it.

v365 Never allow yourself to envy others, for you will lose sight of the truth that way.

v366 Even though you have very little in the world, if you use it wisely and live your life with purpose, people will praise you.

v367 The seeker is no longer dependent on name and form. This makes him indeed a seeker.

v368 The seeker who meditates on love and who follows the way of the Buddha with joy will reach Nirvana.

v369 Empty your boat, seeker, and you will travel more swiftly. Lighten the load of craving and hatred and you will reach Nirvana.

v370 There are five bonds which the seeker must loosen. These five are selfishness, doubt, false values, craving and hatred. Turn these five away and in their place will come five more – longing for this world of form and longing for the formless world, self-centredness, mental purposelessness and ignorance. Transcend these five too and then welcome another five to stay with you – confidence, energy, awareness, concentration and insight.

v371 Make your mind steady and strong. Meditate deeply or you may swallow the red-hot iron of suffering.

v372 If you do not meditate, how will you gain insight? And if you have no insight, how will you concentrate? But if you concentrate with insight, you will come near Nirvana.

v373 The seeker is happy who has a quiet mind and who follows the way.

v374 To reflect on the beginning and ending of things fills the seeker with happiness as he sees the boundless joy of worlds beyond worlds.

v375 First of all the seeker must guard his senses, be calm and follow the right instructions.

v376 The seeker should try to find good friends along the path and learn to put an end to sorrows.

v377 Even as faded leaves drop from the tree, so must craving and hatred fall away from the seeker.

v378 A seeker who is calm in body, calm in speech, calm in mind and has turned away from the worldly, is seen to be a source of peace.

v379 Look to your own nature which is intrinsically pure and rouse yourself. Look to the purity on which the world is founded and correct yourself. Look within and find happiness.

v380 You are the master and you are the way. Where else can you look? As a merchant breaks in a noble horse, so you should master yourself.

v381 The seeker who has confidence in the way will go beyond the way and find the end of suffering.

v382 The seeker who goes beyond the way enlightens the world, just as the moon shines as it passes from behind the clouds.

26 The Enlightened

v383 With all your strength, struggle against the torrent of craving. Let the elements of your being dissolve and realize the truth.

v384 With meditation and concentration, your insight will dissolve all the fetters that bind you.

v385 Free from all the bonds of existence, you will become enlightened.

v386 Meditate, do your work attentively, and live in quietness. The one who lives thus is indeed a sage.

v387 The sun shines by day and the sage in his wisdom shines. The moon shines by night and the sage shines in meditation. But day and night, the enlightened shine in radiance of the spirit.

v388 The true sage has given up harmful thoughts and his life troubles no one.

v389 If somebody strikes you, do not resent that one. He will feel shame, but worse shame would come to you if you showed hatred for your attacker.

v390 The sage who is in control of his thoughts and deeds is at a great advantage. As he avoids violence, so he will come near the end of his suffering.

v391 Never offend in anything you say or do.

v392 Celebrate the one who has awoken. Celebrate the fire of his sacrifice and learn from him the way.

v393 Neither matted hair, nor noble birth, nor caste makes a wise man, but the truth and integrity with which he is blessed.

v394 The matted hair and rough clothing of the recluse do not benefit him if he is of evil mind. He may seem outwardly serene but he is darkness within.

v395 He is a sage who meditates alone in the forest and overcomes his craving.

v396 A man is not enlightened because of his birth status. It is only the one who is free from craving and who possesses nothing that reaches enlightenment.

v397 He is indeed a sage who has cut all the ties that bind him. He has gone beyond fear and is infinitely free.

v398 The true sage has cut the strap of craving, the thong of hatred and the rope of delusion and has transcended all the obstacles.

v399 The enlightened will receive insults with patience and bad treatment with calm, for patience is as forceful as an army.

v400 The one who is free from anger and who keeps promises and has let fall all longings, has conquered himself and lives in this body for the last time.

v401 He is a master from whom pleasures fall like droplets from a lotus, or mustard-seed from the point of a needle.

v402 He is a master who has come to the end of suffering in this life and has laid down his burden.

v403 He is a master who understands the path and knows what to do and what to leave undone. His wisdom brings him to the end of the way.

v404 The sage is content with a simple life and wants little. He does not stay in a house but neither does he beg from others.

v405 He hurts no creature and neither kills nor urges others to kill.

v406 He is peaceful among the violent and free from longing among those filled with craving.

v407 Craving and hatred and envy have fallen away from him as a seed slips from the point of a needle.

v408 His speech is kindly and truthful to everyone he meets.

v409 He takes nothing that is not given to him, whatever its value, size or beauty.

v410 He wants nothing in this or any other world and freedom is his.

v411 Wanting nothing and understanding everything, he is free from doubt and knows Nirvana.

v412 He has gone beyond judgements of good and evil, gone beyond the longings and sufferings of the senses.

v413 He no longer craves for existence in any of the worlds. He has gone beyond time and shines like the moon, clear and spotless.

v414 He has journeyed through many births and deaths and has reached the other shore, free from craving and free from doubt.

v415 Letting go the longing for worldly life and letting go the craving for sensual pleasures, he is now a homeless one with no abode anywhere.

v416 The chain of births and deaths is behind him and so is craving.

v417 No fetter can hold him now, either in this world or the next.

v418 Craving has left him and will never return. He is calm and his energy has overcome all the worlds, both inner and outer.

v419 He has come to know the meaning of birth and death. He no longer longs for either and is now an enlightened one.

v420 He has taken an invisible path beyond the tracing of gods or men and now, by virtue of his purity, he is enlightened.

v421 In him there is no more clinging to name or form or time. He possesses nothing and wants nothing.

v422 He is an awakened one who is fearless and exalted. He is a great sage, has vanquished all things and is an enlightened one.

v423 He is at the end of the path. He sees the flow of his many lives and he sees what the suffering of hell is and what is the perfect joy of heaven. Now birth and death are ended for him and he has done all that should be done. He has reached Nirvana.

Bibliography

Dhammapada, translated by Venerable Acharya, Maha Bodhi Society, Bangalore, 1966

Dhammapada, translated by Dr C Kunhan Raja, The Theosophical Publishing House, Madras, 1956

Hymns of the Faith (Dhammapada), translated from the Pali by Albert J Edmunds, Open Court Publishing Co, 1902

Minor Anthologies of the Pali Canon, Pt 1, *Dhammapada*, re-edited and translated by Mrs Rhys Davies (President of the Pali Text Society), Humphrey Milford, 1931

The Buddha's Way of Virtue, a translation of *The Dhammapada* from the Pali Text by W D C Wagiswara and K J Saunders, John Murray, London, 1912

The Dhammapada, edited by Jack Austen, The Buddhist Society, London, 1949

The Dhammapada, text in Devanagari with English trans-lation by Professor N K Bhagwat, MA, Buddha Society, Bombay, 1935

The Dhammapada, rendered by Thomas Byrom, Wild-wood House, London, 1976

The Dhammapada, Vol X, Sacred Books of the East, translated from the Pali by Max Muller, Oxford University Press, Oxford, 1924

The Teachings of the Compassionate Buddha, edited by E A Burtt, The New English Library Ltd, 1955